How to Manage
Your
Whole Language Classroom

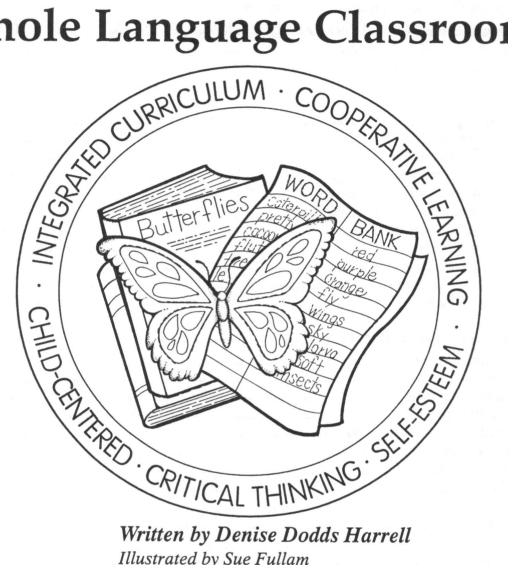

Written by Denise Dodds Harrell
Illustrated by Sue Fullam

Teacher Created Materials, Inc.
P.O. Box 1214
Huntington Beach, CA 92647
©1992 Teacher Created Materials, Inc.
Made in U.S.A.

ISBN 1-55734-144-3

Table of Contents

Introduction

How to Manage Your Whole Language Classroom is an 80-page teacher resource book. It contains two major sections. The first, "Characteristics of a Whole Language Classroom," describes the integral aspects of these classrooms. The characteristics are in no specific order since all are equally important. The brief explanation with each is designed to make the teacher aware of the reasons for putting them into practice.

The second major section, "Components of the Instructional Day," delineates practical "how to's" for implementing the whole language philosophy in day-to-day teaching. Hands-on activities accompany many of the components.

Also provided are suggestions for scheduling, planning a thematic unit and creating a classroom atmosphere conducive to whole language learning.

How to Manage Your Whole Language Classroom provides:

- a definition of whole language

- an explanation of the characteristics of a whole language classroom

- an explanation of the components of the instructional day with hands-on activities

- suggestions for scheduling your instructional day

- tips for planning a thematic unit

- ideas for setting up a classroom environment conducive to whole language learning

- answers to questions often asked by teachers about whole language

What is Whole Language?

Whole language is a philosophy about how children learn. It is a commitment to keep language whole (natural) so that it is learned for its original purpose—to express and receive ideas. Children learn best when language arts—reading, writing, listening, and speaking—are interconnected.

Whole language teachers believe that children should be interacting with materials, the environment, and other classmates while learning. Therefore, whole language classrooms are busy and productive. In this warm, accepting environment, children are in control, free to make choices about their learning, and willing to risk making errors.

Children, parents, and teachers should recognize that learning takes place continually. Therefore, whole language emphasizes the process of learning rather than the end product. In addition, because each student is at a different place in the learning process, teachers should do their best to treat students individually when giving them classroom responsibilities, building their self-esteem, and assessing their comprehension of the curriculum.

Characteristics of a Whole Language Classroom

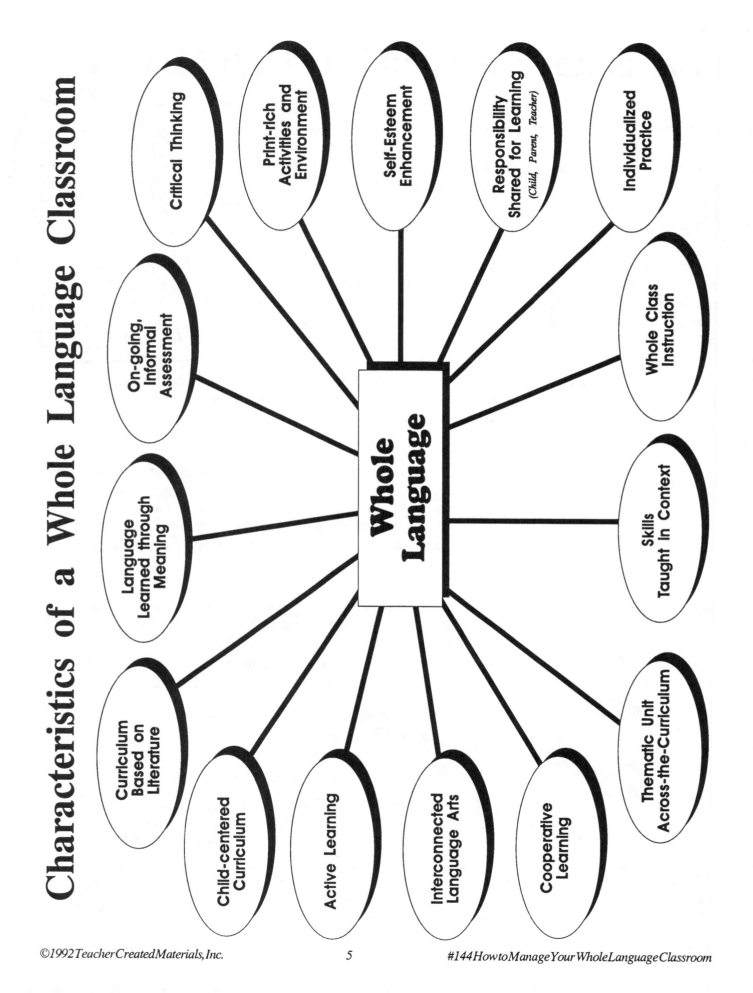

- Critical Thinking
- Print-rich Activities and Environment
- Self-Esteem Enhancement
- Responsibility Shared for Learning (Child, Parent, Teacher)
- Individualized Practice
- On-going, Informal Assessment
- Whole Class Instruction
- Language Learned through Meaning
- **Whole Language**
- Skills Taught in Context
- Curriculum Based on Literature
- Child-centered Curriculum
- Active Learning
- Interconnected Language Arts
- Cooperative Learning
- Thematic Unit Across-the-Curriculum

Language Learned Through Meaning

The natural purpose of language is to communicate.

The complex task of learning to talk is accomplished naturally rather than through deliberate instruction because the learner is surrounded by people who are using language meaningfully.

Children become literate in much the same way they learn to speak. They learn because they want to participate and make sense of the language around them. Making and correcting their own mistakes becomes part of the learning process.

Teachers need to keep the language whole. Traditionally, in early education, language has been taken apart and turned into words, syllables, and isolated sounds. By breaking language up into bite-size pieces, the meaning is lost.

Reading is a constructive process. Skilled readers begin by making a guess about the meaning of parts of the text based on their prior knowledge and experiences about the topic. They look at the print and use available language cues, like pictures or story context. Doing this confirms or changes their prediction about the meaning of the text.

Teachers should have students read entire sections of text when using this natural, whole-to-part strategy. Children naturally break the language down to understand the parts, but this occurs only after they understand the initial meaning of the text.

6

Curriculum Based on Literature

The most effective tool for teaching language in a whole language classroom is quality literature. Books, poems, and the lyrics of songs provide examples of proper written language and serve as the impetus and model for oral language as well. Literature exposes children to natural language patterns and important ideas. Children begin the literacy process by acquiring a love of books. Then, they grow to understand that books are filled with meaning to be comprehended. Last, children discover and unlock the mystery of print.

Printed words were written to say something. They were not written to teach reading skills. Books which control vocabulary and restrict phoneme use (often known as basals) can make learning to read for meaning difficult. Children need selections which express the whole idea if they are to learn to understand print.

Quality literature should be present throughout the entire instructional day. Selections should relate to a theme, and be of various genres and difficulty levels. They should be used as the basis for formal, whole group lessons. They should also serve as vocabulary builders and enrich students by introducing new knowledge and skills.

Child-Centered Curriculum

Children are natural learners. From birth they have sought to make sense of their world. They are constantly experimenting, solving problems, and testing hypotheses to add new learning to what they already know. Whole language classrooms seek to provide a natural atmosphere in which this active, constructive learning can continue. The whole language program respects students for who they are, where they come from, how they talk, and their experiences. Its atmosphere is non-threatening, supportive, and warm. Children are encouraged to take risks without fear of failure.

In the child-centered whole language curriculum, students take responsibility for making choices that will meet their learning needs and allow them to practice what they have learned effectively. By accepting responsibilities and working toward their own goals, they asssume ownership of their learning which fosters their independence.

Whole language teachers have many responsibilities for facilitating student learning. The teacher is responsible for making optimum use of all resources to motivate students to learn. Teachers arrange the classroom environment, provide creative materials, invite participation in class activities, and plan cooperative learning opportunities which integrate several subjects. All sensory modalities—visual, auditory, kinesthetic, and tactile— need to be included in creating the language learning environment. The teacher collaborates with students, gives feedback in the form of questions, allows students time to reach their own conclusions, and models appropriate behaviors.

Active Learning

In traditional classrooms, the teacher is active while the student is the passive recipient of information. Whole language philosophy, however, believes that students learn best when they play an active role in the learning process. When students participate in hands-on activities and interact with their peers, they are more likely to reach their own conclusions through asking questions and testing their ideas.

The opportunity to experiment with language, respond to literature, and design their own creative projects is crucial for students. Ultimately, active learning gives students a sense of ownership and involvement in their experiences and effectively facilitates their desire to learn more about the world in which they live.

Interconnected Language Arts

Children are born with a natural desire to acquire language. Listening is the language skill which is acquired first. It provides a foundation for other aspects of language development. A large portion of all communication time is spent on listening. Secondly, children learn to speak because their powerful natural desire to communicate drives them to learn oral language. Likewise in whole language classrooms, students learn to read and write because there are real reasons to do so.

All modes of communication are interconnected throughout the day in a whole language classroom. Being exposed to and immersed in listening to oral language naturally causes reading behavior to emerge. Children come to see that writing is simply "talk" written down. This talk (or ideas) needs to be verbalized before writing. Reading is comprehending the ideas of a writer. The child's meaningful interactions with the environment are blended with reading, writing, listening, and speaking.

Just as children gradually become secure and proficient as speakers with lots of different opportunities to use language, so too will they become secure and proficient readers and writers. As they read and write to learn, the goal is for students to feel as secure with print as they do with speech. Teachers need to create a literate environment and learning activities across the content areas which will provide language experiences incorporating listening, speaking, reading and writing. (For suggestions on how to do this see Integrated Language Arts, pages 31-36.)

Thematic Approach

When planning thematic units for whole language instruction, be sure to integrate the content areas (science, social studies, health, etc.). Since the day is integrated, the curriculum will not be dissected into separate subject areas. The language arts—reading, writing, listening, and speaking—will be woven throughout your content area lessons. Likewise, your language arts lessons will be based on literature with storylines involving content area concepts. Quality literature lends itself naturally and richly to the development of real-life science, social studies, and other subject area concepts.

The following activity integrates many science, social studies, or other content area topics with the language arts.

Flip Back–and–Forth Book

1. As part of your curriculum, teach lots of information and read many related books on a particular subject.

2. With the whole class, brainstorm facts that have been learned on the topic. Record responses, modeling correct usage and spelling and reinforcing vocabulary.

3. Cut 18" x 3" strips of plain paper. Have each student stack four strips.

4. Fold strips in half and place a rubber band around the fold to make a book.

5. Develop a sentence frame with the students that relates to the topic being studied. For example: *I know that bears* _____.

6. Write the sentence on the cover.

7. Have students complete the sentence frame in a different way on each page. For example:
   > ... *live in the woods*
   > ... *are big.*
   > ... *sleep in the winter.*

8. The book is read by flipping back and reading the front cover before reading each new page.

Skills Taught in Context

The nature and versatility of thematic teaching and integrated instructional days creates the opportunity for many skills to be modeled, taught, and reinforced. In this way, whole language teachers teach skills when students have a reason to learn them in the context of the integrated lesson. Skills are not taught in rigidly set sequences or because the class has reached a certain page in a textbook. Skills are more readily internalized when practiced in context, rather than drilled in isolation.

Children want to learn listening, speaking, writing, and reading skills which will enable them to communicate clearly and accurately. These can be taught in whole group or small group situations by doing hands-on activities. In addition, it is the teacher's responsibility to ensure that skills are practiced and applied independently on an on-going basis.

Ways to teach skills in context are discussed throughout this book, especially in the section called Components of the Instructional Day—Integrated Language Arts (pages 31-36). Be aware that children are exposed to skills in reading, writing, listening, and speaking in all curricular areas and activities through teacher modeling and the provision of quality examples.

Whole Class Instruction

In the whole language classroom, teacher-directed lessons should be conducted for a whole class rather than in small groups. Dividing the class into groups decreases the teaching time to which each student is exposed. In addition, substantial amounts of seatwork are necessary to keep students who are not meeting with the teacher busy and quiet (but not necessarily instructed). Whole class instruction, however, assures that all students are exposed to the same curriculum. Students feel equal with one another because they are not separated into groups which are labeled by their abililites.

The teacher must be sure that all lessons and guided discussions have something for all students even though some parts of the lesson may be too easy or difficult for some students. The easy lesson portion gives children of all abilities a boost in self-esteem and a feeling of mastery over concepts, while portions of lessons that are difficult challenge more advanced students. Even students who do not respond at all during a lesson are usually thinking about the topic and learning from the responses of other students. Overall, whole class instruction challenges students of all abilities and nurtures their higher-level thinking skills.

Independent Practice

Independent practice is a natural follow-up to whole class instruction. Lessons are most **effective** if the materials and literature involved are made available to small groups or individuals for further investigation. Students naturally want to practice what has been presented in order to assimilate new information into their current knowledge. They want to **manipulate**, **repeat**, **share**, and **expand** upon the presented materials. Learning is a social **activity**. In most situations the children need classmates (no matter what the level) to bounce **ideas off** and learn from. Always allow ample time and space for this valuable practice.

The teacher provides a multitude of ways to practice. This enables individual needs to be met. Centers can be set up to house the practice materials and activities. Students can then be allowed to choose or be directed to specific centers. They may work there individually or in small groups.

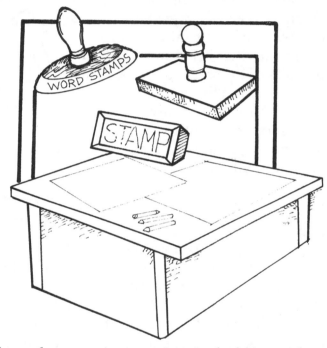

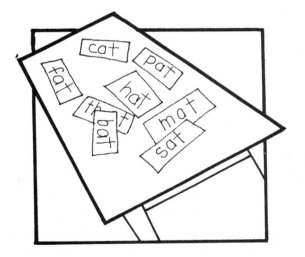

A few other practice exercises include journals and various other kinds of writing, sustained silent reading, rebuilding in the pocket chart, and work with individual word cards. The segment of the day labeled open work time is a time specifically set aside for these activities (see page 46). Remember to allow students to spend several days on one activitiy if they wish since students learn at varying rates and extend their thoughts to different levels.

Literacy skills improve through purposeful practice. Given proper modeling, materials, and guidance along with plenty of opportunities to practice, all students can experience literacy success.

Generic Whole Language Lesson

Follow these steps to create a whole language lesson appropriate to your curriculum.

Step 1
Choose a story, song, or poem with pictures. Read it to your students several times and have the students join in on any part of the text that is repeated. Then discuss, act out, and illustrate the story together as a class to interpret the meaning of the text. These activities bring the words and pictures of the story to life and make it relevant and fun for children. Repeat this step as many times as necessary until children have memorized, or at least become very familiar, with the text.

Step 2
Copy the whole text or repeated sections only onto charts, sentence strips, and/or word cards. Use these to introduce the printed form of the story, song, or poem. If you have used sentence strips or word cards, they can be placed in a pocket chart during this step. As you read and chant the words together, track them with your hand or finger. Do this several times so that students make the connection between each spoken word and its correlating print form. Point out selected phonic elements (e.g., beginning consonant b, short a), word structures (e.g., -ing endings, compound words), and print conventions (e.g., quotation marks, exclamation points). In Step 4 you will study these more thoroughly.

The pig jumped in the mud.

Step 3
Use the story illustrations that were made in Step 1. Match them with the sentence strips or word cards. The children either identify which words go with which picture or the other way around. After the match is made, read and track the words to check for accuracy. This provides additional repetition to reinforce reading skills.

Generic Whole Language Lesson *(cont.)*

Step 4

This step is essential for teaching and reviewing skills such as phonics, punctuation, and vocabulary. While students are looking at the print of the selection you are studying, have them respond to questions like the following examples.

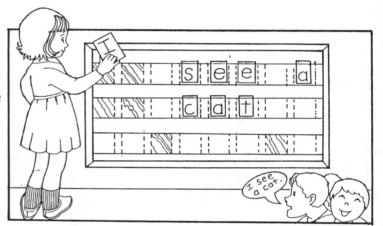

A. Could this be the word *table?* (Point to a word.) Do you see letters in this word that match the sounds you hear at the beginning, middle, and end of table? (Emphasize t, b, and l sounds as you say the word.)

B. What word rhymes with *ball?*

C. What is this word? Can you tell me another word that means the same?

D. Which word tells what size the bear is?

E. What do we call this mark? (Point to a punctuation mark). Why is it here? (Review or teach a quick lesson on the particular punctuation mark you wish to emphasize.)

Step 5

Shuffle picture cards, word cards, and sentence strips and pass them out to students. Recall together what happened first in the story. Locate the appropriate words and pictures and place them in the pocket chart. Continue to rebuild the story in this manner chanting the words aloud together as you go.

Step 6: Independent Practice

- Allow individuals or small groups of students to use the book, pocket chart, and other materials to reenact the entire lesson.

- Give each student a sheet printed with the sentences or selected words from the story. Let each student cut the sentences or words apart and glue them into a book. Have them add illustrations. Students should read and reread their books silently or with a friend.

- Have students rewrite the story by using parts of sentences and supplying new words or phrases to complete them.

Shared Responsibility for Learning

In a whole language classroom, the child holds the primary responsibility for his/her learning. However, the teacher and parents share this responsibility by facilitating and encouraging learning. Without the proper environment and models, the child will not have the tools or the motivation to learn. Since learning takes place at all times, the responsibility for a child's learning must be shared between home and school.

The child's responsibilities are:

- to express ideas

- to work cooperatively with others

- to listen to and accept ideas of others

- to interact with materials, the environment, and others

- to ask questions and seek information and strategies to answer those questions

- to absorb as much language as possible through reading, writing, listening, and speaking

Shared Responsibility for Learning *(cont.)*

The parents' responsibilities are:

- to make the child responsible for daily tasks
- to keep the school-home relationship open and positive
- to spend time reading and listening to the child every day
- to limit the use of electronic devices like TV and video games
- to be knowledgeable about whole language and the way children learn
- to respect the child's independence by allowing adequate time and space for his/her activities
- to model an enthusiasm for learning language by being readers and writers themselves
- to see that the child gets adequate sleep, exercise, and nutritious meals

The teacher's responsibilities are:

- to keep language whole (natural)
- to model an enthusiasm for language and its function
- to create a positive and nurturing environment for students
- to provide a curriculum that is interesting, relevant, and purposeful
- to make encouraging comments which instill a "can do" attitude in students
- to respect students' independence by allowing adequate time and space for their interactions
- to provide and monitor activities integrating reading, writing, listening, and speaking which give students valuable practice with language
- to keep parents informed and involved in classroom happenings
- to raise open-ended questions which will develop students' thinking skills and lead them to make appropriate decisions
- to help students express their difficulties and suggest possible solutions

Self-Esteem Enhancement

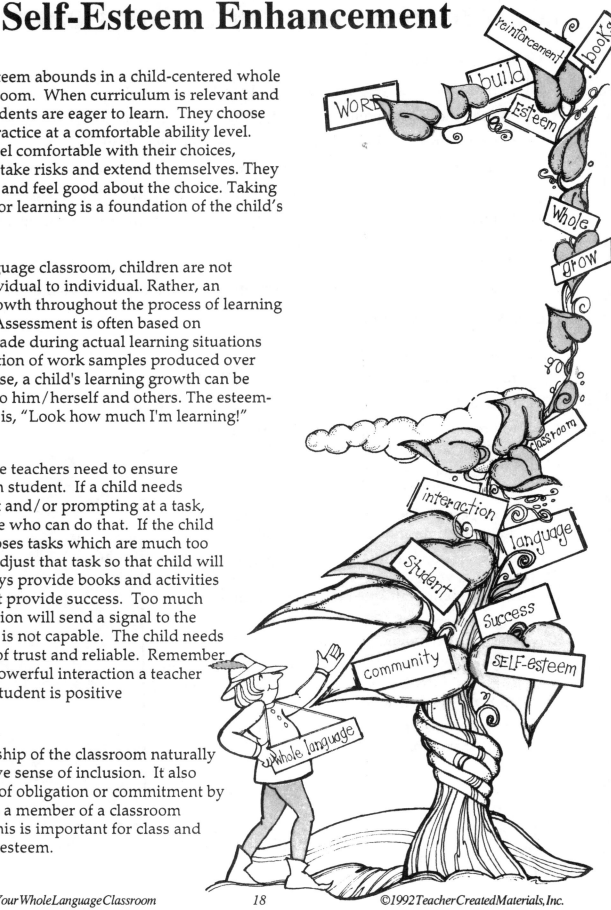

Positive self-esteem abounds in a child-centered whole language classroom. When curriculum is relevant and motivating, students are eager to learn. They choose independent practice at a comfortable ability level. Because they feel comfortable with their choices, students freely take risks and extend themselves. They choose to learn and feel good about the choice. Taking responsibility for learning is a foundation of the child's self-esteem.

In a whole language classroom, children are not compared individual to individual. Rather, an individual's growth throughout the process of learning is recognized. Assessment is often based on observations made during actual learning situations and on a collection of work samples produced over time. Using these, a child's learning growth can be demonstrated to him/herself and others. The esteem-boosting result is, "Look how much I'm learning!"

Whole language teachers need to ensure success for each student. If a child needs encouragement and/or prompting at a task, find a classmate who can do that. If the child constantly chooses tasks which are much too difficult, help adjust that task so that child will succeed. Always provide books and activities to challenge yet provide success. Too much teacher interaction will send a signal to the student that he is not capable. The child needs to feel worthy of trust and reliable. Remember that the most powerful interaction a teacher can provide a student is positive reinforcement.

Student ownership of the classroom naturally instills a positive sense of inclusion. It also creates a sense of obligation or commitment by each student as a member of a classroom community. This is important for class and individual self-esteem.

Print-Rich Environment

The environment of a whole language classroom is highly literate and stimulating. Functional, meaningful, and relevant print is everywhere. Numerous displays throughout the classroom invite the students to read, share, and enjoy. The print found throughout the classroom is "kid friendly." The amount and complexity of print grows with the students and much of it is created by them. Children learn to read by reading and to write by writing, so it is the teacher's job to provide as many opportunities as possible for reading and writing.

Listed below are suggestions for incorporating the language arts throughout the classroom and making the environment rich in printed materials.

- Use labels throughout the room to identify objects and serve as a reference for spelling.

- Provide at least 100 books for a class of 30 children.

- Let the children see that you write notes that serve specific purposes to yourself and others.

- Display pertinent information for the students to read (like lunch menus, reminders, responsibilities for various member of the class, etc.)

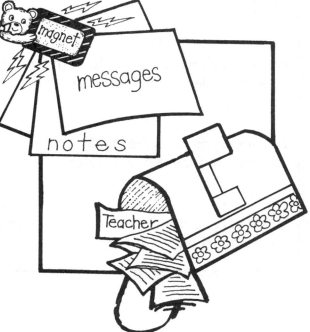

- Display a message board so that notes to the class can be written. For example: "Don't forget your library book Tuesday."

- Provide a mailbox to encourage children to write notes to the teacher.

- Post the daily news that the class dictates and publishes.

- Display books, poems, sentence strips, and songs that have been studied.

- Prominently display students' written work.

Critical Thinking

In a whole language environment, children are given control of their own learning. They are actively asking questions and seeking answers about the world. They are encouraged to use many sources of information to make guesses about solutions and to test those guesses to see if they make sense. When students are given the freedom to think about solutions to problems in a risk-free, non-judgmental environment, they are challenged to think at higher levels. See Bloom's Taxonomy below for a description of the different learning levels.

Teachers must teach and model for students how to think critically rather than only teaching students the "correct answer" to a question. Use Bloom's Verbs on page 21 to help you develop questions that will encourage students to think at higher levels.

Bloom's Taxonomy: Levels of Learning

Knowledge
This level provides the child with an opportunity to recall fundamental facts and information about the story.

Comprehension
This level provides the child with an opportunity to demonstrate a basic understanding of the story.

Application
This level provides the child with an opportunity to use information from the story in a new way.

Analysis
This level provides the child with an opportunity to take parts of the story and examine these parts carefully in order to better understand the whole story.

Synthesis
This level provides the child with an opportunity to put parts from the story together in a new way to form a new idea or product.

Evaluation
This level provides the child with an opportunity to form and present an opinion backed up by sound reasoning.

Bloom's Verbs

The lists of verbs below correspond to different levels of critical thinking. Use them when creating writing assignments or asking children questions. Students' responses will help you determine the level at which they are thinking.

KNOWLEDGE		COMPREHENSION		APPLICATION	
Name	Recall	Explain	Paraphrase	Transfer	Apply
List	Draw	Summarize	Review	Compute	Show
Define	Count	Interpret	Demonstrate	Produce	Change
Match	Identify	Predict	Conclude	Choose	Paint
Label	Sequence	Tell	Generalize	Use	Select
Describe	Quote	Discuss	Locate	Demonstrate	Prepare
Recite	Write	Restate	Identify	Interview	Dramatize
Tell	Find	Illustrate	Report	Draw	Imitate

ANALYSIS		SYNTHESIS		EVALUATION	
Differentiate	Compare	Create	Produce	Judge	Predict
Contrast	Outline	Design	Compose	Select	Rate
Deduce	Characterize	Propose	Invent	Prove	Choose
Classify	Separate	Organize	Pretend	Decide	Evaluate
Debate	Analyze	Construct	Originate	Appraise	Conclude
Research	Discriminate	Develop	Integrate	Rank	Assess
Distinguish	Examine	Plan	Rewrite	Criticize	Justify
Relate	Diagram	Make Up	Perform	Prioritize	Argue

Question Mark Pattern

Use this pattern as a template. Trace around it on brightly colored paper and cut out the question mark. Write some of Bloom's verbs on it. Use them for writing or oral discussion. Or, select a question word (who, what, where, why, how), pose a question, and allow students to think about and express their thoughts. Students will come to see this symbol as a signal to "put their thinking caps on."

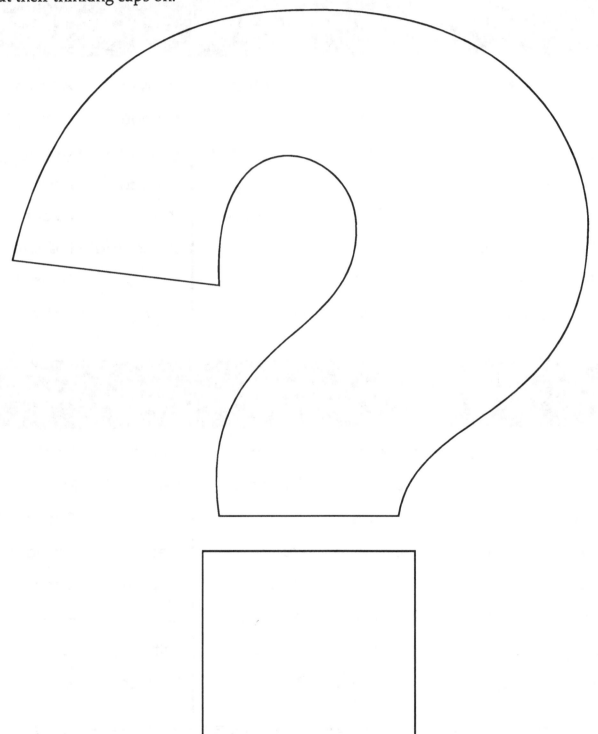

Cooperative Learning

Since learning language is a social activity, group interaction is an essential component of a whole language classroom. Group activities should be a regular part of school life. Students need to learn social skills as well as academic skills. Cooperative groups can accomplish both.

Cooperative learning groups should be composed of small numbers of students of mixed abilities. In the planning for these groups, teachers should consciously include social objectives. Before beginning group work, students should understand the social, as well as the academic objective (s). As part of the assessment of the effectiveness of group work, the teacher should monitor the quality of the group interactions. A variety of instructional methods, materials, and modes of output should be encouraged so that all group members can find a way to express themselves.

A major component of the language arts is listening. This is a skill that must be developed and is imperative to learning since most instruction from teachers and classmates is oral. Group situations require members to actively listen to the speaker, understand what has been said, possibly restate what was said, and finally interpret that message in order to respond to it.

Cooperative group experiences have valuable outcomes. Children get a sense of inclusion. Students feel that they are expected to participate and that the group provides a safe environment for doing so. This makes it easier to voice opinions and take risks.

The practice in reading, writing, listening, and speaking that occurs in cooperative groups is most effective among groups of students of various ability levels. In facilitating an effective whole language classroom, the teacher must encourage and allow numerous opportunities for cooperative learning.

On-Going, Informal Assessment

Assessment in a whole language classroom should be happening continously. New information pertaining to a particular child's strengths and weaknesses will be gained daily. Most of the time, this will occur informally while watching and listening to various children. Attention should be paid to areas that have been mastered and areas where reteaching and additional practice are needed. A means for recording this information should be developed.

It is important to remember that within the philosophy of whole language, learning is process oriented. Students should not be measured (evaluated) based on an end-product. For this reason, keeping records and samples for each individual child is imperative. These can be referred to by teachers and parents when assessing that child's growth toward literacy. The most effective way to keep this type of necessary information is through the establishment of a portfolio for each student. (See Teacher Created Materials #145 *Portfolio Assessment for Your Whole Language Classroom* for more information.)

Whole language classroom teachers have specific skill objectives; however, they are not always sequential in nature. As soon as a skill has been taught and ample practice has been provided, students should be evaluated for mastery. Keep in mind that since skills are integrated and overlapping, child-centered curriculum implies that some students will learn a skill sooner than others.

Furthermore, literacy is not easily broken down into measurable skills. Instead, it is a complex building of numerous concepts and abstract thinking processes and should be considered as such when evaluating student achievement. For example, if a child is able to accurately read and understand a selection, it becomes irrelevant whether or not he/she can give the sound of the letter b in isolation.

Oral Language Activities

Primary students arrive in the classroom bursting with something to share. Starting the instructional day by allowing each student to speak to a caring audience sets a supportive, positive tone for learning.

Allow students a few minutes to hang up wraps and unpack book bags. After students have reported to their seats, promptly start the following activity. At first many students will not be prepared to participate quickly, but eventually all students will.

"Snap Clap" Oral Response Chant

1. The teacher poses a question that will require more than a yes or no answer. (For example: "Are you buying lunch or did you bring it today?")

2. The teacher and the students begin this snap-clap pattern in a rhythm:

   -slap *(both hands slap lap once)*
   -clap *(both hands clap once)*
   -snap *(right hand)*
   -snap *(left hand)*

   The teacher calls on a specific student while "snap-clapping." (slap; clap; "Su"-snap right hand; "sie"-snap left hand) (Susie)

3. Student responds by answering the question in a complete sentence. ("I brought my lunch to school today.")

4. The teacher immediately restates the child's response, modeling correct grammar if the student has made any errors. ("You brought your lunch to school today.")

5. The teacher follows steps 1-4 calling on each student.

6. Two questions may be asked of the students at the same time, with responses given one after the other. Ask questions that require complete sentence responses.

   If a child has difficulty responding due to language barriers or shyness, the teacher may have to provide an answer for the child to repeat. The child will have another opportunity tomorrow to answer on his/her own. No attention is called to improper grammar or wild comments.

   The entire class snap-clap chant should last about 5-10 minutes. As the year progresses, the chant can go faster and become more complex.

Oral Language Activities *(cont.)*

Calendar

Daily calendar activities are an excellent way to develop oral language as well as numerous math skills. Calendar exercises are best done with the whole class participating in the chanting and singing while one child, who is the calendar leader for the day, does the manipulation. Use a large bulletin board for your calendar display. Be sure it is visible to all students and low enough for a child to use.

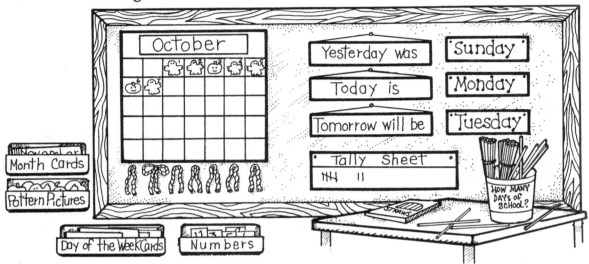

Choose from the activities below. Vary them from month to month.

- Display a blank month calendar. Make appropriately shaped cutouts to fit in its squares. (For example, you may wish to use pumpkins and ghosts for October.) Each day give a different child the opportunity to add a pattern piece and write the day's number on the calendar. Establish a pattern for the cutouts. (For example: ghost, ghost, pumpkin; ghost, ghost, pumpkin.) As the pieces are added each day, the pattern can be recited and the shape of the next day's cutout predicted.

- Display the months of the year in order. Recite or sing these with the leader pointing to appropriate month labels. (See Bibliography, page 80 for suggested records.)

- Make and hang labels: *Yesterday was; Today is;* and *Tomorrow will be.* Have the calendar leader add the appropriate day of the week after each. Then lead the class in an oral recitation of the completed sentences. The month and number can be added to make the sentences more complex.

- Staple the center of a 12" piece of yarn under each day of the week. Have the calendar leader tie a bow under the appropriate day of the week.

- Display a number line from 0-31 for use in counting up to today's date.

- Post a piece of construction paper labeled as the tally sheet. The calendar leader adds a tally mark each day (diagonally slashing each fifth one and circling each group of ten).

- It's fun to keep track of the number of days in school by adding a straw to a container each day. (Many classes work toward a celebration on the 100th day of school!) Model and teach that when 10 ones are together, a bundle or a "ten" can be made, and ten tens make 100.

Oral Language Activities *(cont.)*

Secret Letter Detective

This oral language activity is a guessing game that reinforces letter recognition and phonics, gives responsibility, boosts self-esteem, and engages students in critical thinking and cooperative learning.

Prior to introducing this activity, make the secret letter necklaces and reproduce the parent letter (page 28) that accompanies the necklace when it goes home.

Next, decide how often you'd like to incorporate this activity in your schedule (every day, every other day, or once a week). The activity takes about 5-10 minutes to complete depending on the maturity of the class and the difficulty of the item the detective has chosen. Children will be eager for a turn so devise a way to manage selection of the detective. Making it one of the classroom jobs is an easy way to accomplish this.

Preparation: When you introduce the secret letter necklace to the class, model how to use it and explain exactly what is expected when it is returned. Each time a child takes home a secret letter necklace, send the accompanying parent letter. Be aware that you may need to take a child aside, help find an item in the classroom, and think of three clues if parent support at home does not exist.

Cut posterboard into 3" squares. Punch a hole near the top center. Insert a 3' piece of craft yarn and knot to form the necklace. Write a different letter on each in dark permanent marker. Store on low hooks so students can choose their own.

Student directions:

1. Take the necklace and note home.
2. Find something that contains that letter's sound.
3. Think of three clues that will help the class guess what it is.
4. Hide the item in a container so that it remains a secret from all members of the class.
5. During oral language activities, stand on the speaking platform (see page 72):

   • Show and identify the letter to the class.

   • Identify all the sounds that the letter makes in this word and others. The class echoes the sounds.

   • Tell where the sound occurs in the word that names your object—beginning, middle, or end.

   • Give the first clue.

   • Watch the second hand on the clock for one minute so that the class has ample time to think.

   • Choose a child by name. Listen to the guess. Tell him or her if it is correct. If it is not, choose another classmate to guess. Listen to three guesses before giving another clue.

   • This is repeated until the item is guessed or the detective has given three clues and received three guesses for each clue.

   • If no one can guess, the child remains secret letter detective for one more day.

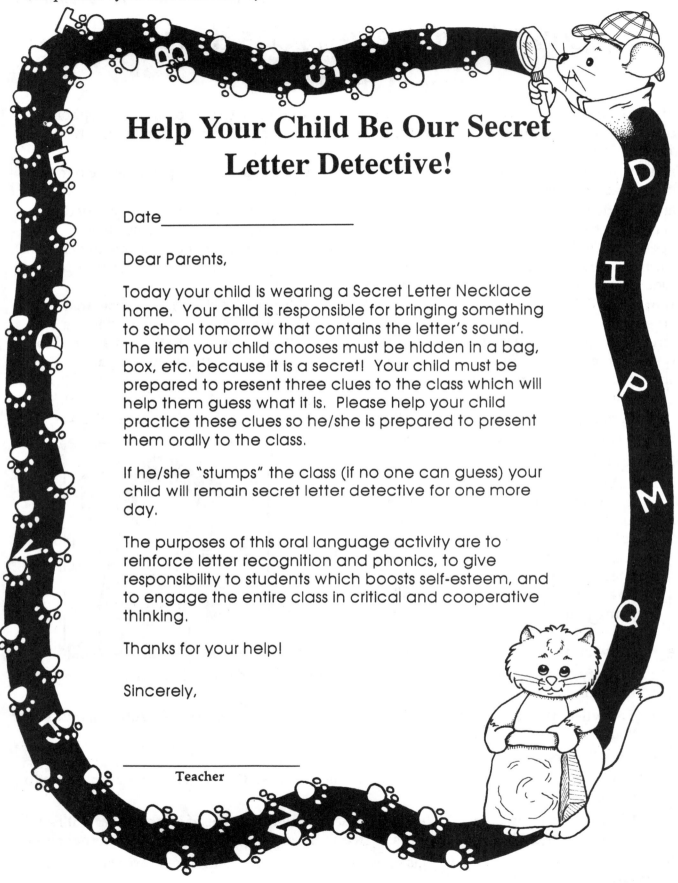

Help Your Child Be Our Secret Letter Detective!

Date_____

Dear Parents,

Today your child is wearing a Secret Letter Necklace home. Your child is responsible for bringing something to school tomorrow that contains the letter's sound. The item your child chooses must be hidden in a bag, box, etc. because it is a secret! Your child must be prepared to present three clues to the class which will help them guess what it is. Please help your child practice these clues so he/she is prepared to present them orally to the class.

If he/she "stumps" the class (if no one can guess) your child will remain secret letter detective for one more day.

The purposes of this oral language activity are to reinforce letter recognition and phonics, to give responsibility to students which boosts self-esteem, and to engage the entire class in critical and cooperative thinking.

Thanks for your help!

Sincerely,

_____
Teacher

Oral Language Activities *(cont.)*

Word Walking

Word Walking is a fun activity for use in practicing and reinforcing sight words or vocabulary words. These words must have been taught in context prior to practicing the words in isolation.

Directions:

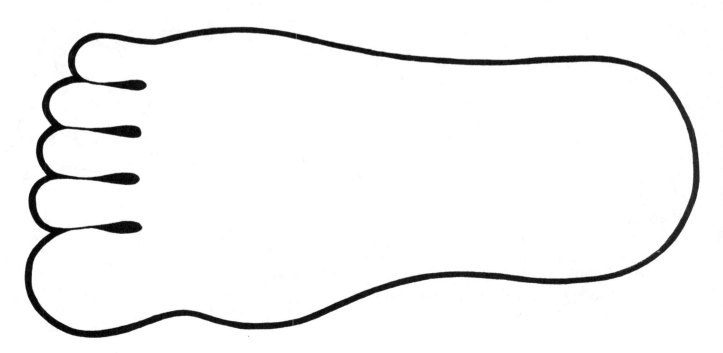

1. Make a tagboard pattern of the foot below.

2. Trace around the pattern several times on construction paper. Turn the pattern over and trace an equal number of times to make left feet.

3. Cut out.

4. Using a thick marker, write a word on each foot. Use an equal number of left feet and right feet.

5. Cover with clear, adhesive paper on both sides.

6. To play, instruct students to place footprints on the floor and read the words aloud as they are walked over!

7. As extensions, arrange the words in sentences or have students put them into alphabetical order and walk over them.

Reading

Sustained Silent Reading

Sustained Silent Reading (S.S.R.) is an activity that should be expected every day of all individuals in the classroom. Everyone chooses a book and stays engaged in reading it for a sustained length of time. It is important for students to realize that they are capable of this and that reading can be a form of recreation. This also gives students an opportunity to practice individually what they have been taught.

To facilitate Sustained Silent Reading, the teacher should explain and model the following rules:

- Each individual selects one book. (Make available all kinds of books; no trading of books during reading is allowed.)
- Each individual reads alone silently. (Realize that younger students tend to subvocalize as they read.)
- Adults in the classroom also choose a book and read uninterrupted.

Set a timer to signal the end of S.S.R. Start at five minutes and gradually increase to fifteen minutes or more depending on the maturity of your class.

Partner Reading

Another effective and fun form of reading practice is partner reading. This is a time when students pair up with a classmate or a cross-age buddy to read books of their choice together.

Allow more time for partner reading than for silent reading since time for socialization is necessary. This is a wonderful time for friendships to be established. Encourage positive reinforcement and taking turns.

Some strategies for this include:

- Study and discuss the illustrations, then together choose the illustration that is the best, scariest, silliest, etc.
- Together find the longest word, ten compound words, other words that mean big, etc.
- Read the book taking turns by sentences or pages.
- After sharing the book, ask each other one comprehension question.
- Choose a character and tell your partner why you'd like to be that character.
- Tell your partner why you like or don't like the book.

Integrated Language Arts

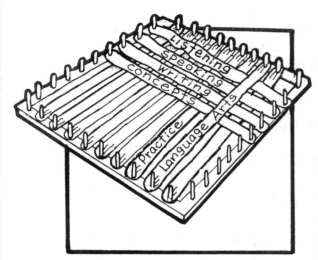

No longer is a period of the instructional day labeled reading because all strands of the language arts are integral and interconnected. Reading is not an isolated subject that is experienced independently. Learning language is social, thus utilizing listening, speaking, and writing, as well as reading. Hence, the label language arts is more accurate. Furthermore, reading is more than just decoding words; without context and prior experiences, words are meaningless. Therefore, during this part of the instructional day, teachers will be instructing and facilitating practice in all the language arts. Remember, too, that this chunk of time will incorporate themes and concepts taken from the other content areas such as science and social studies.

Within the context of your thematic unit, plan a whole-group, integrated language arts lesson each day. (See pages 54-61 to help with planning.) This lesson should have all four language arts components as well as some relevant, motivating content in it. It is also imperative that your lesson(s) focus on some whole piece of text. It can be selected literature, a song, or a poem.

Integrated Language Arts *(cont.)*

These steps should be followed when using a piece of literature with children.

Get Into the Literature: Provide background experiences and activate students' prior knowledge. To do this you might choose one of following activities:
- Arouse interest in the story by reading aloud to the group related literature selections that will add to student's conceptual background.
- Relate the topic to personal experiences.
- Provide a hands-on concrete experience, like a field trip, a demonstration , or observation of actual artifacts.
- Brainstorm what is already known about a topic to enable students to learn from each others' knowledge and experiences.
- Show a related video, film or filmstrip dealing with the topic.
- Conduct a related science experiment.
- Role play social situations that might instigate certain feelings which will make the topic or subject more relevant and familiar.

Go Through the Literature: Work with a piece of literature by focusing on meaning and language. In order to accomplish this:
- Share the pictures only. Tell any information you get from the illustrations; make predictions about story content.
- Guide the reading of the selection—students read a section and then teacher reads it with the students and discusses it.
- Teach the vocabulary within the context as the class reads the selection.
- Read the selection through echo reading—teacher reads a line, then students echo (read) the same line.
- Read the selection together and identify parts of the story—characters, setting, plot, etc.
- Read the selection together and discuss it from different characters' points of view.
- Build and rebuild all or part of the story in the pocket chart.
- Read the selection and make up comprehension questions to answer in cooperative groups.

Go Beyond the Literature: Extend and build students' knowledge through discovery and practice. Some activities to accomplish this include:
- After reading the selection and working with the print, relate the literature and issues to the students in some way. These beyond activities should build on what the students know and cause them to stretch their thoughts and experiences.
- Rewrite the story making some change in a story part.
- Dramatize the selection.
- Write a response in your journal about the selection.
- Role play being a specific character.
- Do a book review on the selection.
- Create an art project related to the selection.
- Make up a song.
- Find a related recipe and cook it.
- Make a Big Book.

Integrated Language Arts *(cont.)*

Word Banks

Word Banks are collections of related words. They are frequently used and displayed in whole language classrooms. Creating and manipulating a word bank provides an excellent opportunity for integrating reading, writing, listening, and speaking. Word Banks are created by brainstorming with groups of children. Children build on each other's ideas as they link their prior knowledge with new learning. Brainstorming to create word banks is a meaningful and profitable activity.

As the class brainstorms words children already know about a topic, they are recorded by the teacher on the chalkboard, chart paper, butcher paper, or individual word cards. The words should be printed large enough to be easily read by students and should be hung in a place that is easily seen. As ideas are recorded, model and discuss skills and strategies for decoding the word. State each word as it is written so that students can see the connections between speech, print, and spelling/phonics. Tie together the speaking, listening, reading, and writing by stating, "I heard you say _____. This is how it is written and then we can read it." Write the word, say it slowly, and call attention to any phonetic rules that apply.

During this time, large amounts of vocabulary are developed. Each addition to the word bank should be discussed thoroughly. This causes the children to expand or alter their background knowledge and will aid them in manipulating the word bank words. It will also help in using these words accurately in writing and speaking.

Word Banks should grow. Whether the collection of words relates to a theme (topic) or is based on a skill (for example, a compound word bank), it should belong to the children. Words should be transferred to individual cards and illustrated by the children so that the cards can be manipulated. They should remain accessible to the children during open work time, journal writing, or other writing activities.

Integrated Language Arts (cont.)

Word Banks (cont.)

Manipulation of word banks must occur in a group situation, large or small. This enables students to share ideas, learn from each other, expand or alter the particular schema they have, and develop confidence and friend-making socialization abilities.

Arranging the word banks into categories makes the words meaningful and causes children to defend their positions and think abstractly. Skills and confidence are gained by such activities. For these types of activities, the words must be on individual word cards. An illustration on each card is extremely helpful. The individual cards can be manipulated in a pocket chart, on the floor or large table area, or on the chalkboard using reversed masking tape strips. Remember, for the greatest value the word bank should remain available for the students to use in practice and as a reference when writing.

Organizing a group of related words into categories can be done in many ways. Any way is correct as long as the student has an acceptable reason for sorting this way. Categories may include choosing a structural feature of the word (like words with -ing ending), putting the words into alphabetical order, grouping according to conceptual attribute (large animals, small animals) or organizing by largest to smallest word. Note: When sorting into categories, be sure to ask "What's the rule for sorting?" or "Why do these words go together?" Give ample thinking time.

Integrated Language Arts (cont.)

Pocket Charts

Pocket charts are valuable tools for teaching and learning in a whole language classroom. They may be purchased at teacher supply stores or ordered from many school product catalogs. They contain clear, plastic pockets through which word cards, picture cards, and/or sentence strips can be seen. Pocket charts make an attractive display for word banks, poems, songs, etc. and help create a print rich whole language environment. The words can be used in writing assignments or copied for handwriting practice. Thus, pocket charts are excellent for the integration of the language arts. And, perhaps most importantly, pocket charts provide for easy manipulation of words by students for valuable practice in group or individual situations.

The pocket chart can be utilized very effectively to focus an integrated language arts lesson. The words to a poem, song, or repeated portion of a story can be placed in the chart. Lines of text are clearly separated enabling students to "track" (follow along with finger) easily. This aids the child in discovering phonics and the reading-writing connection. Use large, heavy-duty recloseable clear plastic bags to store words and sentences from recent lessons near the pocket chart for students' individual practice. Pocket charts provide for the important shared reading experience. The use of large words in the chart with the students gathered around reading together allows students to see the print and hear the sounds of the language just as in the lap-reading done by many parents even before kindergarten. This is important to reading readiness and is difficult for teachers to give to each student individually.

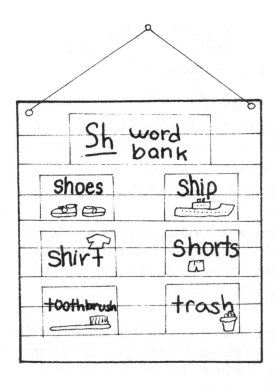
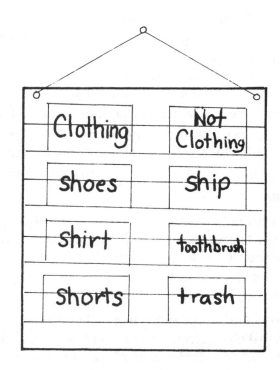

Integrated Language Arts *(cont.)*
Big Books

Research shows us that a common experience of most good readers is that they were read to as young children. Typically, a child sits on the parent's lap, viewing the pictures and text, while the parent reads. The child's attention is focused on the illustrations and the print as the book is read aloud. Teachers have always read to children, but most children cannot see the text or illustrations clearly during these reading sessions. Big Books are a way to involve groups of children so that they form an understanding that the process of reading is print stimulated.

A good shared or "read together" Big Book should have several of the following characteristics:

- Natural spoken language
- Predictable story line
- Rhyme and/or rhythm

- Repetition of phrases
- Illustrations that capture the children's interest
- Print that is big enough to be seen easily by children from a distance of four meters (13 feet)

The shared Big Book experience has four main components. They are as follows:

1. Discovery and Predictions

Discovery includes setting the stage for the first enounter with the story and the illustrations. This can be done by recalling or providing related background experiences. Predictions about the book set up a framework that is confirmed or changed as the story is read. Children learn to become active readers, which is a key to successful reading.

2. Exploration and Conventions

By exploring and studying the conventions of the printed Big Book page, children learn the skills required for reading and writing. This includes phonics, punctuation, vocabulary, or any other conventions of writing. To help children master the basic process of reading, the teacher can use such techniques as:

- Encouraging responses and asking questions about the story.
- Pointing to each word as the book is reread. (This step is crucial in the early grades.)
- Asking questions about the format of the printed word such as: "Where do we begin on a page?" "Which way do we go?" "Why are there blank spaces between words?"
- Pausing before a predictable word and allowing the children to fill it in.

3. Extensions

Rewrite and reillustrate the story with the children, act it out, and/or discuss the sequence of the story. Make or purchase matching little books to use with individuals or small groups. Use the story as a theme for a whole language unit. This unit can extend across the curriculum to cover math, science, art, music, poetry, movement, cooking activities, etc.

4. Independence

Place Big Books and accompanying little books (commercial, teacher or child-produced) in the classroom for all children to experiment with and use for independent reading or recreational browsing. Record the stories and place the tapes and books at a listening center. Provide an opportunity for children to check out the books and take them home overnight.

Spelling/Phonics

Understanding the phonics of our print system is crucial to both reading and writing. In working toward the goal of helping students to become more successful writers and readers, spelling and phonics must be addressed. Writing is the natural way to explore the phonics of language. Frequent writing will do more to increase spelling achievement than any other single activity because it helps the student to discover the function of phonics and the way words are put together.

At the beginning, students must practice writing with their attention focused upon meaning rather than the correctness of their spelling. To get children to write frequently and take risks with written language, encourage and accept "invented" or phonetic spelling. As children work with pocket charts and Big Books and increase their word recognition, they will self-correct their invented spellings. This is a developmental process that occurs naturally in a print-rich environment where children read and write frequently.

Correct spelling of high frequency words is learned both through applied practice in reading and writing, and through direct spelling instruction. Direct spelling instruction should occur at all grade levels but in a limited amount—about one hour per week is maximum. High frequency words often are not phonetically written and must be internalized through repeated use. (See page 73 for a sample list of words that are frequently used in writing.)

Strategies for teaching spelling include:

- Use the Try Sheet (see page 45) while journal writing.

- Circulate among students as they are writing, calling attention to misspelled words.

- Use individual lap chalkboards for teacher-guided lessons. Students say the words slowly, becoming aware of how their mouths move, hearing their sounds in sequence, and then recording that sequence on the chalkboard. High frequency words whose meanings are understood should be practiced using the following strategy:

  1. Teacher says the word.
  2. Students repeat the word.
  3. Teacher uses the word orally in the context of a sentence.
  4. Teacher writes the word correctly on the overhead projector or chalkboard.
  5. Students copy the word correctly on individual chalkboard.
  6. Students look at the word carefully as the teacher says the word.

(continued on next page)

Spelling/Phonics *(cont.)*

7. Students continue looking at the word as they say it.

8. Students trace over each letter with their fingers as they spell the word orally.

9. Students completely erase chalkboard.

10. Students rewrite the word from memory.

11. Immediately, the teacher spells the word correctly so students can check and correct if necessary.

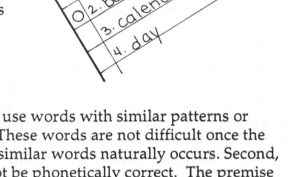

Alphabet activities can teach phonics and spelling. Any activity that attaches letters with sounds or entails an analysis of word structure is good practice. (See pages 40 and 41.)

The more traditional practice of utilizing word lists for practice and eventual mastery is a legitimate strategy. Be sure that practice with the spelling/ phonics words occurs in some meaningful context before they are practiced in isolation.

These lists can include three types of words. First, use words with similar patterns or phonograms (like *cat, sat, flat,* or *king, ring, wing*). These words are not difficult once the pattern is internalized and generalization to other similar words naturally occurs. Second, include frequently used words that may or may not be phonetically correct. The premise behind this is that these words have been practiced and applied many times before. Last, be sure to include some theme words pertaining to the literature and topics currently being studied. These word may be challenging.

When initially assigning a word list, administer a pre-test to establish which words have already been mastered. Use the First Try Spelling on page 39 for this. Students should correct this pre-test themselves under teacher supervision. This leads to self-motivation and achievement.

Dictation

Dictation sentences are an effective bridge between spelling and daily writing. They should include only spelling words that have been mastered. Before giving the dictation sentence, signal for the children to listen. Then, recite the whole sentence. The children repeat the whole sentence out loud before they are allowed to write it. The teacher repeats the dictation sentence only once while students are writing. Have the students touch each word as you repeat them one last time after they have finished writing. Provide a model for the children to use to check their work. This can be written on the chalkboard or overhead projector, or the teacher may have prepared sentence strips to place in the pocket chart. Be sure they understand and check punctuation as well as spelling.

First Try Spelling Test

	My First Try	Correct Spelling	Need to Practice
1.			
2.			
3.			
4.			
5.			
6.			
7.			
8.			
9.			
10.			
11.			
12.			
13.			
14.			
15.			

Spelling Sheet

Draw and label 2 pictures that begin with "F" and 2 pictures that begin with "B".

F f	B b

Print your words.

_____

_____

_____

_____

Practice the letters.

F _____ f _____ B _____ b _____

My Alphabet Dictionary

_____
(theme/topic)

Write a word for each letter.

A a is for _____	**B b** is for _____	**C c** is for _____	**D d** is for _____
E e is for _____	**F f** is for _____	**G g** is for _____	**H h** is for _____
I i is for _____	**J j** is for _____	**K k** is for _____	**L l** is for _____
M m is for _____	**N n** is for _____	**O o** is for _____	**P p** is for _____
Q q is for _____	**R r** is for _____	**S s** is for _____	**T t** is for _____
U u is for _____	**V v** is for _____	**W w** is for _____	**X x** is for _____
	Y y is for _____	**Z z** is for _____	

Modeled Writing/Daily News

One of the most functional and relevant activities to share with a class is modeled writing. Students need to see the language arts being put into practice. Also, it is imperative that students see proper handwriting, sentence structure, grammar, spelling, and vocabulary used in an exemplary manner. Both of these important tasks can be accomplished by leading the class daily in a short modeled writing.

With all or part of the class assembled close and able to see the writing surface, record students' dictation as they watch. The writing surface can be the chalkboard; however, since these sentences need to be copied later, an easel with a large pad of paper or a laminated piece of chart paper with an erasable marker may be preferable.

The class can discuss the news of the classroom, locality, state, or world, and with your guidance come up with group dictated sentences. They can take turns giving you sentences to write or, after stating several sentences, collectively decide which ones will be recorded. Alternatively, the teacher can choose sentences that you know are relevant to the students that day.

Slowly and carefully record the sentences being dictated. Use neat handwriting, correct grammar, vocabulary that is understandable to the students, and the necessary conventions of writing (capital letters, periods, apostrophes, etc.). These conventions should be explained simply and matter-of-factly while writing. After writing each sentence, read back what has been written. Be sure the class can read it.

The dictated sentences should be copied by the teacher, a partner, an upper grade tutor, or a student in the class for keeping permanently. They can be copied on plain paper or in newspaper format (see page 43) to serve as a newsletter from your room. Choose a student or two to illustrate the sentences daily or at the end of the week. Duplicate a copy for each student and send it home to parents. The children should read and reread these significant events from your classroom.

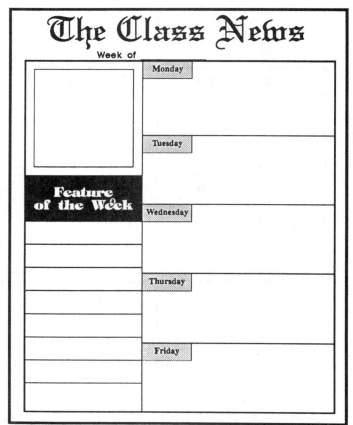

Class News and Review

The Class News

Week of _____

| | Monday |
| Tuesday |
Feature of the Week	Wednesday
	Thursday
	Friday

©1992 Teacher Created Materials, Inc. 43 #144 How to Manage Your Whole Language Classroom

Journal Writing

Journal writing should be used at all grade levels to encourage writing. It is an integral part of whole language curriculum that gives students freedom to write on whatever topic interests them. Students become more confident and fluent writers as a result of this.

During journal writing time it is quite useful for the teacher to circulate throughout the classroom discussing students' journal entries with them. Comment positively on something that is good , but also cite one thing that can be improved. Be sure that whatever item or skill you are pointing out is at an understandable level to that student. Simply mention a correction, explain the reason why, and encourage the student to correct it.

Later take the time to read what your students have recorded in their journals. Write a brief reply to the student. This reply should be in response to the content.

Your Try	Teacher	Write the word again correctly

Use Try Sheets (page 45) with your class. These will cut down on the inevitable question, "How do I spell this word?" Before students write in their journals, have them take out their Try Sheets. As they get to a word they're not sure how to spell, have them write it in the Your Try column. As you circulate around the classroom, look at the Try Sheets and write the word correctly in the Teacher column. If the student has spelled it correctly, put a happy face in this column. The student then copies the word correctly in the last column. Limit them to one or two words a day. In this way they can learn the correct spellings.

Journals are an assessment tool since they give teachers valuable insight into their students' strengths, weaknesses, and interests. They also illustrate growth in a student. For this reason, students should be encouraged to date each entry. At parent conferences, share journals to illustrate students' status and progress. You may wish to institute a policy where students are allowed to fold over pages that they do not want to share. Be sure you keep their trust.

Name_____

Try Sheet

Your Try	Teacher	Write the word again correctly

Open Work Time

Open work time is provided every day for independent student practice. During this time, everyone is engaged in learning by interacting with an activity.

It is important to allow students to choose which activity they'd like to further discover and manipulate. Some will choose the same activity for several days if their curiosity is stimulated or if they're becoming expert at the task, which in turn builds their self-esteem. Students tend to choose activities appropriate to their ability level because activities which are too easy or too difficult will not hold their interest. If a child is not able to choose an activity which is appropriate or productive, you may have to provide guidance.

This block of practice time is quite useful in assessing students. Teachers can hear and see what students are choosing, what they are capable of doing, what they are interested in, and how well they get along with others.

The teacher needs to provide many types of activities. He/she must also give instructions, model them, and set specific parameters for the use of each. Teachers must also be able to explain the various skills and purposes for each activity for visitors and/or parents who experience this time with the class.

Once the classroom is conducive to productive, enjoyable learning, the teacher's job is simply to monitor behavior. When students are involved and active, take the opportunity to listen and watch all of the excitement that learning brings to the classroom.

There are many areas or activities that can be made available to the class during open work time. (See pages 42 - 49 for specific suggestions). Remember to provide activities done previously in formal instruction. Repeating lessons and activities is quite a useful learning tool for students. Lower achieving students benefit from the repetition while higher achieving students will improvise and extend the learning.

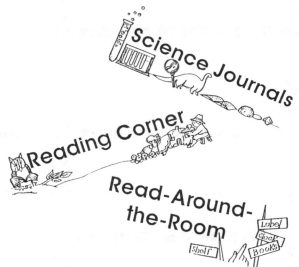

The labels provided on pages 47- 49 can be duplicated and used during open work time to mark each area or activity. Duplicate each twice—use one to label the area or activities and one to display as either opened or closed. Using a pocket chart or double sided masking tape, put up the labels of the areas that are open. Hang this in a place that is easily seen. The second label can be hung or placed at the area that is open for work. Children can match words or pictures to find out which areas are available. Labeling the centers open or closed gives the option of closing an activity that is being used inappropriately or needs some update or adjustment.

Finally, open work time should not be used as a reward for finishing a particular task or for good behavior. It is a fundamental part of the instructional day for each student. Students will find an activity they can perform successfully somewhere among the choices.

Open Work Time Labels

Chart-Rebuilding

Art Center

Games/Puzzles

Open Work Time Labels *(cont.)*

Read-Around-the-Room

Science Journals

Reading Corner

Open Work Time Labels *(cont.)*

Alphabet Area

Publishing Center

Listening Area

Reading Aloud

Reading aloud is the single most important activity for building the knowledge for eventual reading success. Reading aloud makes reading a pleasurable experience instead of a chore. As adults read aloud, children see positive reading role models, gain new information, are exposed to books, and experience the emotions elicited by the literature. Reading aloud to children must be a part of every elementary teacher's daily program. The frequency and length of read-aloud sessions will vary according to the maturity level of your students. Be aware that every minute of this time is valuable as it stimulates imagination, stretches attention span, improves listening comprehension, nurtures emotional development, and establishes the very important reading-writing connection.

When reading aloud to your class, remember to:

- Use words like "title," "author," "title page," "publisher," etc. when introducing books.
- Read the same books over and over again.
- Include old favorites as well as a new book every day. Occasionally read books with a richer vocabulary and a more complex story line than most of your other read-aloud books.
- Include fairy tales in your collection of read-alouds. Read several different versions of the same fairy tale.
- Invite a more able student or another adult to read aloud.
- Have a world map near your read-aloud area. Point out where particular stories originate or are set.
- With some selections, discuss setting, characters, main idea, plot, etc.
- Don't underestimate the children's attention spans.
- Read many kinds of writing including poetry, newspapers, and magazines.
- Read slowly enough for the child to build a mental picture.
- Bring authors to life by learning and sharing some personal information about them.
- Add an interesting dimension to read-aloud time whenever possible by bringing in something authentic pertaining to the story.
- Read just for the enjoyment of experiencing a good piece of literature.

Math

The foundations of mathematics instruction in your whole language classroom should be similar to the whole language philosophy. The curriculum should be child-centered and based on discovery learning. For math concepts to be meaningful and thus internalized, the activities must be process-oriented utilizing thought rather than rote memorization.

As with learning the system of print in our language, math instruction must have the child at the center of the activity. The effective math teacher stimulates the student to learn by serving as a model and a guide as the child uses math manipulatives and functional, real-life objects to discover our number system. Patterns and order in number, relationships among them, and likenesses and differences in mathematical properties are gained through process skills and thinking activities.

Problem solving and logic, which are major parts of the math curriculum, should be modeled and discussed by the teacher with many whole group and/or cooperative group experiences followed by individualized practice and application.

Integrate math concepts and activities with literature. This can be accomplished by making children aware of math concepts as they are found in literature. As you read, point out the uses of numbers, measurement, geometry, and problem-solving found in stories. Tell children in advance what math concepts to look for. Talk about these when you have finished reading. Extend this by developing sample problems based on the literature.

Fine Arts: Music, Drama, Art

Whole language welcomes the fine arts—music, drama, and art—as an integral part of the curriculum and a vehicle for language. Lessons and activities integrating the arts should be a fundamental part of the integrated whole language day, not merely extra-curricular or enrichment projects.

Music

"Chanting" (rhythmically reciting poems, songs, and text) is a form of music that is integrated in most whole language lessons. Children need to hear the rhythm and rhyme of our language. "Feeling" the text is an effective and alternative mode for children to experience literature.

Songs are a wonderful means of teaching additional vocabulary and concepts around a theme. They make the integrated language arts section of the day enjoyable, meaningful, and child-centered. If related music is selected for a theme and sung repeatedly to the point of memorization, teachers can take advantage of the internalized meaning by presenting the print that accompanies that song or chant. This can be in the form of a large chart, a Big Book, a child-made book, or sentence strips. Furthermore, songs can be rewritten with the children's ideas and words. Then the new text is put in print, practiced, and illustrated. This instills an appreciation of song writers and personal identification with them.

Drama

In primary whole language classrooms, drama is inevitable. When working with a piece of literature, children and teachers cannot avoid expressing its meanings and feelings. Dramatic expression is an excellent way to disseminate meaning to students who do not already have prior knowledge on which to attach the new meaning.

Whole language teachers must make an effort to ensure plenty of dramatic expression during formal lessons and individual practice. Some suggestions include retelling, mime, puppets, masks, and plays. Even children who are less able to read the print can understand the meaning and express it in great detail using one of these suggestions.

Drama is a valuable tool to use before the literature to build prior knowledge or after the literature to review its themes and content. Attending plays and shows and viewing videos are quite useful to build understanding and background knowledge.

Fine Arts *(cont.)*

Visual Arts

The very important visual arts are often the easiest and most motivating to whole language students. Providing many varied artistic experiences is imperative. And relating these experiences to a theme or piece of literature is a means to integrate the language arts.

One formal strategy utilizing the visual arts is that of a guided art lesson. In a guided art lesson, a leader (an artist, a student, a teacher) guides the students in a step-by-step procedure to recreate an art project. Information regarding the subject must be provided prior to the lesson using as much language in the instruction as possible. Attributes are discussed at great length as the students are following the leader's example with theirs. This is an excellent lesson in vocabulary as well as artistic process.

During a guided drawing lesson, the leader may use the chalkboard, easel, or overhead projector. As students draw along, make sure they understand that this is only a practice time to experiment with the elements of drawing (line, shape, color, shading, etc.). Immediately, allow a few minutes for individual, private practice with what they have just learned. Lastly, apply this important guided art lesson to a more refined art project.

Music, drama, and art are fundamental parts of the curriculum and are imperative to your thematic plans. These types of activities are usually easy to include in the integrated day. Activity books, teacher manuals, and fellow teachers are plentiful for brainstorming fine arts lessons. Whenever possible, include reading, writing, listening, and speaking with these types of projects.

Sample Plan

Level: Beginning First Grade Theme: Colors		
Activities	**Time**	**Subject**
Lunch tally with "Snap-Clap" game Calendar activities Oral question: "Are you buying or did you bring your lunch?" and "What is your favorite color?"	8:25-8:45	**ORAL LANGUAGE**
Review S.S.R. rules Allow 3 minutes to choose a book Set timer for 7 minutes	8:45-9:00	**SUSTAINED SILENT READING**
Mary Wore Her Red Dress by Merle Peek (Group Activity); *Jesse Bear, What Will You Wear?* by Nancy Carlstrom; *My Shirt is White* by Dick Bruna Sentence strips for *Mary...* (words; picture cues) chant together; choral reading Distribute copies of *Mary...*; study, discuss art	9:00-9:45	**INTEGRATED LANGUAGE ARTS**
Distribute chalkboards Recite words-kids repeat words and attempt to spell (on chalkboard) by writing sounds they hear in the order they hear them Model correct spelling Kids write it again correctly	9:45-10:00	**SPELLING/PHONICS**
	10:00-10:15	**RECESS**
Group discussions of yesterday's science lesson on mixing colors Take dictation of a few sentences from children Discuss conventions (punctuation, etc.) and phonics as sentences are written	10:15-10:30	**MODELED WRITING/ DAILY NEWS**
Distribute individual journals Write on chalkboard: Today is September 10, 1992. Students copy this sentence into journal Write a word or sentence (s) and illustrate	10:30-11:00	**JOURNAL WRITING**

Sample Plan *(cont.)*

Activities	Time	Subject

Open Areas:
    Listening Center
    ABC Activities
    Art Area
    Science Observation Area
    Reading Corner
    Introduce and model "Read-Around-the-Room"
	11:00-11:30	**OPEN WORK TIME**

Pick up from open work time. Choose 5 volunteers to read today's journal entries to classmates (on stage).	11:30-11:40	**PREPARE FOR LUNCH/SHARE**
	11:40-12:30	**LUNCH**
New theme books to introduce and read: *The Mixed-Up Chameleon* by Eric Carle and some *Ride a Purple Pelican* poems by Jack Prelutsky. Be sure to read some old favorites, asking discussion questions.	12:30-1:00	**READING ALOUD**
Using hands-on math strategies, conduct free exploration with: Unifix cubes; pattern blocks; colored pasta; teddy bear counters; beans; jewels	1:00-1:55	**MATH**
	1:55-2:05	**RECESS**
P.E.: Play "Red Light, Green Light"; Red=Stop; Yellow=Walk; Green=Jog "Traffic Director" holds up different colors and students follow directions for the colors. **Music:** Sing with Big Book "I Can Sing a Rainbow"; Sing "World Is a Rainbow" and track words on chart	2:05-2:30	**PHYSICAL EDUCATION or MUSIC**
	2:30-2:40	**PREPARE FOR DISMISSAL**

Flow Chart for Planning a Thematic Unit

Thematic units are an excellent way to use whole language teaching. Focusing on a theme helps integrate all the subject areas. Use the charts and forms on pages 56- 61 to help you plan for thematic units.

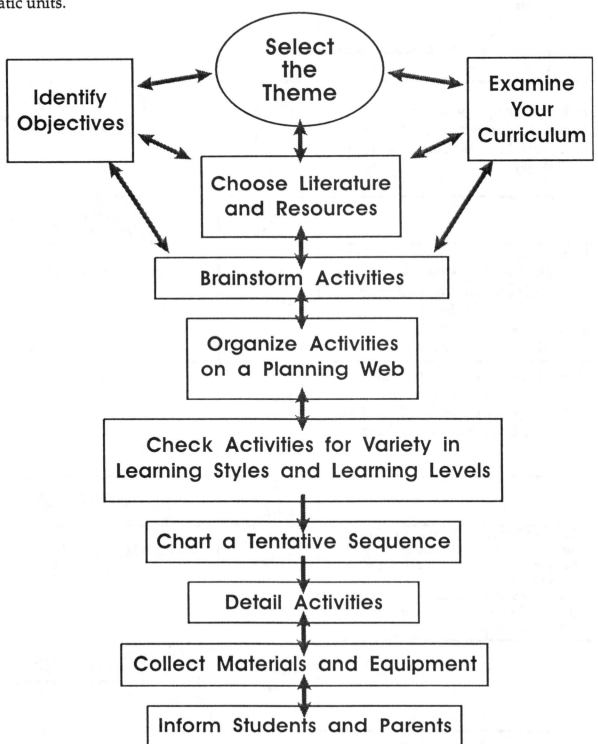

Flow Chart for Implementation of a Thematic Unit

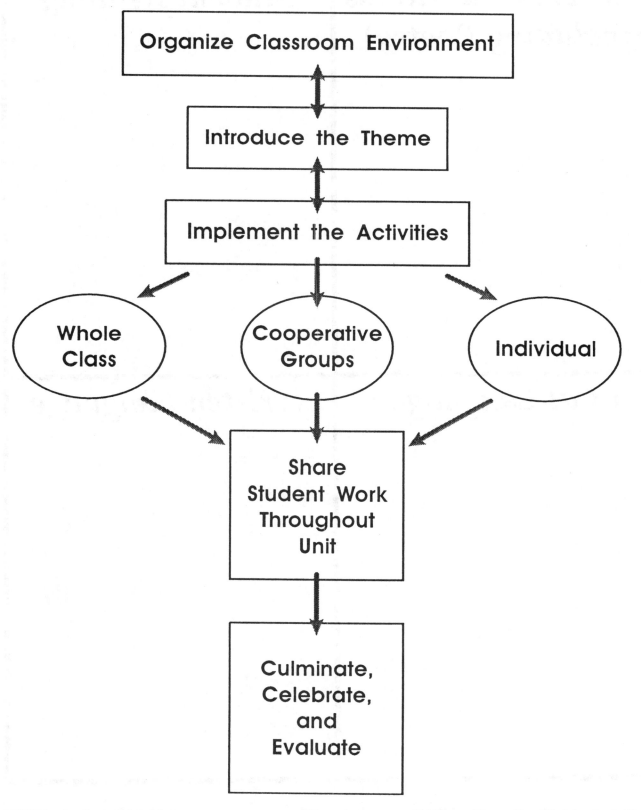

Brainstorm Form for Unit Activities

Teacher Read Alouds (including Poetry)	*Student Reading*
Oral Language	*Written Language*

Brainstorm Form for Unit Activities

Science	*Social Studies*
Math	*Physical Education/ Movement*

Brainstorm Form for Unit Activities

Art	*Music*

Culminating Activity

60

Planning Web

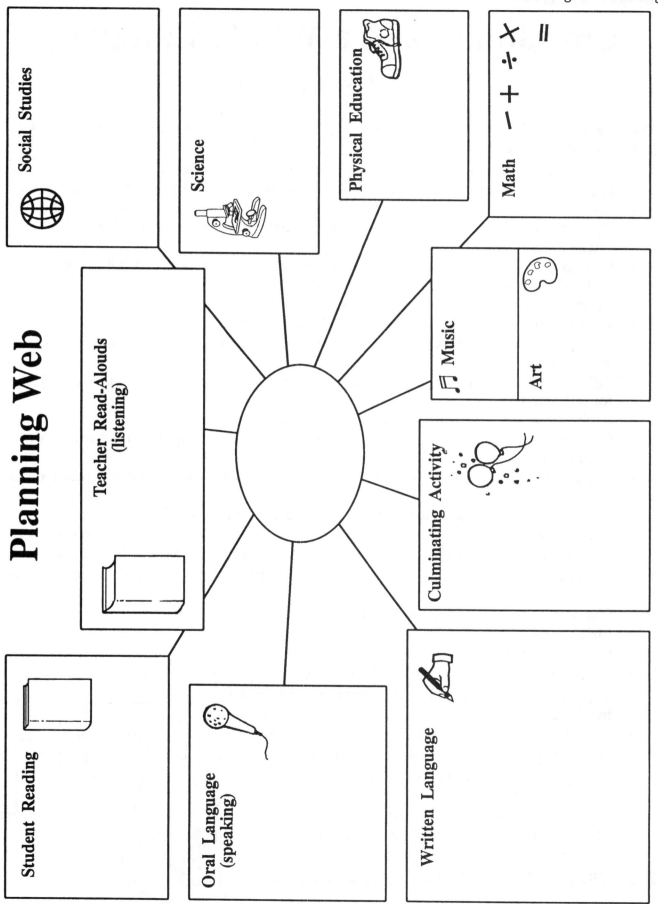

- Social Studies
- Science
- Physical Education
- Math
- Music
- Art
- Culminating Activity
- Teacher Read-Alouds (listening)
- Student Reading
- Oral Language (speaking)
- Written Language

Components of a Whole Language Classroom

When planning and setting up a whole language classroom environment, use the following list of important components as a guide.

- Work space for each student (tables or desks arranged in clusters)
- Place (desk, cubbie, supply box, etc.) for students to store supplies for which each is responsible
- Open space where entire class can gather on floor close to the teacher for group activities
- Chalkboard (at group work space) large enough for group brainstorming, recording, and modeled writing
- Teacher's personal area (desk, cupboard)
- Area for students' backpacks, wraps, etc. (closet, hooks)
- Book corner, class library, and/or interest book baskets where numerous books are available to students
- Publishing company with all kinds of reference books and supplies used exclusively for publishing
- Alphabet area with books, games, letters, and stamps
- Storage area for paper (lined writing paper, plain unlined paper, extra papers from prior lessons)
- Word Bank area (large chart paper) displayed low enough for students to read and add to
- Science Observation area located away from individual work space
- Art area with organized supplies (media, stencils, art tools) and art instruction books
- Feature author bulletin board with space for storage of collection of author's works
- Display area for accurately formed alphabet letters and accompanying "Dictionary-on-the-Wall" words
- Physical education equipment storage
- Listening area
- Computer area
- Speaking platform and space for its storage near open group work area
- Big Book storage (rack on wall or large laundry basket)
- Individual chalkboards and erasers (socks) and storage
- Teacher file cabinets and storage space (boxes, closets)
- Stand for pocket charts for student manipulation
- Large bulletin board, wall space, or clothesline
- Calendar bulletin board
- Bulletin board for class information
- Message bulletin board near entrance to classroom
- Student responsibility (job) bulletin board
- Student of the week (VIP) bulletin board

Library/Reading Corner

A reading corner or library is imperative to your classroom. It should be cozy and completely accessible to all students. A set of shelves or several receptacles filled with all kinds of books is the basic ingredient. You can collect books from book clubs, school and public libraries, and thrift stores. Don't forget to include student-authored books as well as the books on which you have based previous lessons. Be sure to make available books of various reading levels, from picture books and wordless books to more difficult ones.

A cleanable bean bag chair and/or pillows with washable pillow cases are wonderful to have for kids to feel at home in their library. Add a stuffed teddy bear so that students always have an "ear" in which to read.

Art Area

Integrating art with reading, writing, listening, and speaking is a wonderful way to get children motivated and engaged actively in learning language. Analyzing characteristics and details in order to draw requires high level thinking skills and refined eye-hand coordination. When children choose to use the art area, encourage the addition of labels, words, and/or sentences to the art they create.

In this area you should provide many different supplies and tools with which kids can create. Listed below are suggestions:

- crayons
- washable markers
- colored pencils
- scissors
- glue sticks
- stencils (letters and pictures)

- shapes to trace around
- step-by-step art instruction books
- real photographs of items pertaining to your theme
- an easel with paints
- construction paper (other paper is available in paper cart)

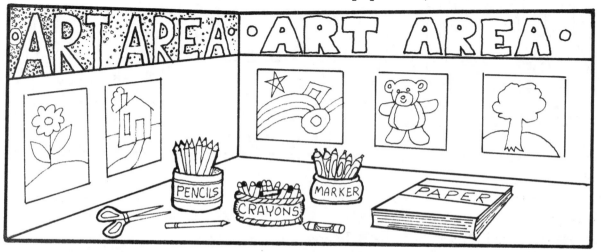

Publishing Company

"Publishing" student-authored books is highly effective in boosting their confidence as writers. It also makes the writing process relevant in the children's lives; they realize that authors are real people and that they themselves are capable of being authors.

Setting up a Publishing Company is not difficult, and it can be used continuously with little maintenance. Choose a location in your classroom with a small partition for display of a Publishing Company sign (a small bulletin board or poster). Be sure the location has ample counter or table space for the following:

- A supply of pre-made books for publishing (directions on page 65)

- A receptacle(s) for crayons, colored pencils, markers, pastels, and letter stencils or rub-on letters for titles; which are to be used as publishing supplies only

- Space to display already published books.

- Space for storage of books as writing references, like dictionaries (at all levels), word books, etc.

Publishing Company *(cont.)*

Obtain manuscripts (stories) for publishing from journal entries, creative writing assignments, or stories written by individual students during open work time. Be sure that all students at all ability levels periodically publish books.

For less able and ESL students, simply take dictation using the following method and allow them to illustrate. After the students have selected what to publish, meet with them to print their words in a blank book. As the students read the manuscript to you, repeat and write their ideas making them grammatically correct, while keeping ideas as near to the original words as possible. Write a sentence or two on each page using a dark pen. Be sure to edit spelling, punctuation, etc., as you re-write the story with the student watching. Guide the student-author in deciding on an appropriate title for the book which reflects the main idea of the story. Finally, before allowing the student to illustrate the book, have him/her practice reading it to you.

Directions for Making Books for Publishing

Materials for each:
  one 9" by 12"/ (22 cm x 30 cm) piece of construction paper
  3 or 4 pieces of 8 ¹/₂" by 11"/ (21 cm x 28 cm) ditto paper
  stapler
  book tape or colored plastic tape about 2" (5 cm) wide

Directions:
  1. Fold construction paper in half.
  2. Fold ditto paper in half.
  3. Place open ends of folded ditto papers in binding (fold of construction paper).
  4. Staple on binding.
  5. Tape over staples.

Alphabet/Alliteration Activities Area

An area containing manipulatives and activities involving the letters and sounds is necessary in every primary whole language classroom. Children who have not reached the level of taking words apart into letters and sounds will be afforded the opportunity to practice these important skills. Students who have mastered letters and sounds will enjoy and extend these activities that "play" with our language. This type of area is also especially effective for ESL (English as a Second Language) students and less able students, who can learn a lot by studying picture books containing alphabet skills.

There are many activities that teach and reinforce use of the letters and sounds. A few suggestions are listed below.

Make available several alphabet, alliterative, and word books for students to study over and over.

Sets of individual alphabet letters and/or pictures with accompanying letters can be purchased or made. They can be made easily by cutting apart appropriate posters or books, such as *David McPhail's Alphabet Book A to Z* (Scholastic, 1989). **Note:** If you choose to cut up alphabet books to make individual cards, you'll need to cut up two, due to the back-to-back nature of these books. Mount these on construction paper so that children are not confused as to which side to use. Lamination increases durability.

Be sure to provide a more challenging set where no letter is displayed and the child must identify the letter by using the picture clue only. The children are experts at creating tasks for using this area to practice. However, here are a few tasks you can model and encourage:

— Put the letters in alphabetical order.

— "Walk" the letters by placing them on the floor and then identifying and stepping on each. Students can name the letter, picture, or another word that has that letter at the beginning or ending.

— After putting in alphabetical order, play "missing letter" with a friend or two. To play this game, one student takes out a letter while other players turn away or cover their eyes. Then students are asked to open their eyes and identify the missing letter.

— Purchase magnetic letters and provide these for students to manipulate. These letters can be used on the side of a file cabinet or on large metal cookie sheets. These areas need to be large enough for more than one student to work.

— Word cards with phonetic words, high frequency words, or "theme" words can be provided with these letters for kids to reproduce and read.

— The same kind of activities listed above can be done using individual letter stamps and ink pads.

Storage Cart

Paper Cart

This three-tiered cart on wheels is for paper storage. It is always available to students at open work time. In it is found:

Lined Writing Paper - A supply of lined writing paper for students to use in creating stories, writing notes to the teacher or to friends, reporting an incident to the suggestion box, etc.

Plain Paper - This can be regular duplicating, plain scrap, or computer paper. Children use this for the art center activities, for stamping out words and sentences with the rubber letter stamps, for stamping out coins with rubber coin stamps, or just doodling.

Extra Papers - This stack is made up of the few papers the teacher has left at the conclusion of a lesson or project. These are very useful and appealing to the student because most of the time he/she has completed this task already. This makes it a great opportunity to repeat a task for reinforcement.

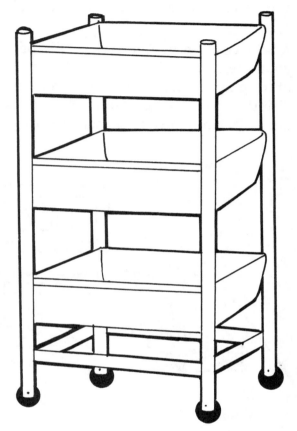

This cart can be adapted to serve as a paper or chalkboard cart.

Chalkboard Cart

Individual chalkboards are necessary for phonic/spelling lessons, guided art, and proper handwriting formation instruction. These individual chalkboards (dry erase boards can be substituted) enable each student to be actively engaged in learning. Students feel free to correct errors without fearing that mistakes will be conspicuous.

Ask parents to contribute old, large cotton tube socks. These make excellent erasers. Chalk can be stored in the toe of the sock. These "erasers" are easily laundered by a volunteer parent about once a month.

Storage of chalkboards is best in a three-tiered cart on wheels. This mobility greatly expedites distribution and collection of the chalkboards.

Science Observation Area

Incorporated throughout your thematic units are many opportunities for real-life science experiments. For example, classroom critters can be learning tools if students are given time and space to observe them and make discoveries about them.

A Science Observation Area should be a part of all whole language classrooms. In setting up your science area, be sure that it is low enough for students to observe without touching or picking up. Model early the "don't touch" and "please touch" types of behaviors. As children visit this area during open work time, expect to hear stimulating conversations and questions among them. Encourage their curiosity, but respect their independence!

Provide Science Observation Journals (see page 70) so students can independently record observations and discoveries. After a time, be sure to be available to assist the class in making conclusions and extending what they've learned in some way.

Books with facts pertinent to the animal, item, or process being observed should be provided for students who are compelled to research more sophisticated information.

Sometimes it is very stimulating to set up a science experiment or add something interesting to the Science Observation Area without a comment from you at all!

Science Observation Journal

Science Observation Journals are an effective way to integrate science and language arts. Students simply record their observations and thoughts or questions about those observations in a journal kept in the science area. The observations may be recorded with words or sketches which keep track of changes both in the science item or in the thoughts and discussions of the students.

Science Observation Journal entries can be completed as a team effort or an individual activity. Be sure to model making and recording observations several times when introducing the journals to the science area.

	Science Observation Journal	
Date	What Was Observed	Observer

Use the student recordings in the Science Observation Journals as a focus for class science discussions. You should lead these discussions and guide with probing questions, but it is not usually necessary for you to give any explanation. Students come to accurate conclusions as a result of classmates' comments and your questioning.

How To Make a Science Observation Journal

1. Cut two pieces of 8 ¹/₂" x 11" construction paper to create a cover.

2. Insert several Science Observation Journal sheets.

3. Staple together and cover stapled edge with book tape.

4. Title it and place in Science Observation Area.

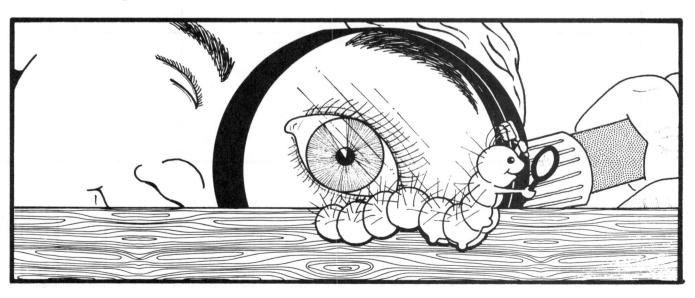

Science Observation Journal Page

Science Observation Journal

Date	What Was Observed	Observer

     70

Listening Area

The listening area is one of the most enjoyed activity choices at open work time. Children listen and sing or follow along in a book together.

In this area, provide a tape player that is easy for children to operate. The tapes with song search (stops between songs) greatly helps children select particular songs. Mark the play button with a green sticker, the stop button with a red sticker, and the rewind button with a yellow sticker. Model for the class proper use of the player, and explain the color code.

Using headphones inhibits the cooperative experience of singing and/or reading together. The use of headphones makes it difficult to hear what the children have chosen. Furthermore, when children impulsively want to sing along or read along, the loud voices of the children with headphones on is quite distracting. Without headphones, hearing the children in the listening area is a pleasant learning sound. Since no headphones are being used, it's important to mark with bright fingernail polish the volume limit line that is comfortable for your classroom environment.

BOOKS HERE

Story BOOK

BOOKS

Story Cassette

TAPES!

Do not store a cassette tape with its accompanying book in a baggy as is traditionally done. Instead, store them separately so that kids are encouraged to read titles of books, or text, and cassette tape labels when they are making a listening choice.

Speaking Platform

In a whole language classroom where reading, writing, listening, and speaking are interconnected through the instructional day, a speaking area is quite useful. If you are lucky enough to have a small stage, use it. If not, you might decide to make a small platform. Make sure that it is sturdy, steady, and mobile.

There are other ways to make students stand apart from the rest of the class while speaking. The easiest is to acquire a large carpet square (3'x3'/1m x 1m) or small area rug. Designate this rug as your "speaker's platform." This can be decorated by adding on some fancy braid, trim, or stars. Anytime students speak in front of the class, have them stand on this special "platform." This can easily be moved around the classroom and be stored in a closet if need be.

Acquiring and using a speaking platform will positively effect your students in the following ways:

- The sharing of thoughts and writings will increase.

- Public speaking skills will improve.

- Listening skills will improve.

- Students will learn to respect the speaker. Student-authored stories will become accepted as more authentic.

- Students will realize that the teacher is not always the person in control of the class.

- Students will be motivated to stand proud and share.

Dictionary-on-the-Wall

The main purpose of "Dictionary-on-the-Wall" is for students to have easy access to correct spelling of frequently used but difficult to spell words. Alphabetizing is an important skill taught through this activity. Students also gain confidence in finding needed information independently and experience repeated practice at correctly writing words that must be memorized.

In order to display a Dictionary-on-the-Wall, a large alphabet (like the traditional alphabet letters displayed above the chalkboard in many classrooms) is needed. A 12" (30 cm) space below or above each letter is necessary for posting words. The location of the alphabet and accompanying Dictionary-on-the-Wall should be central so that children can see to copy the words while writing. Words posted should be those used frequently by the students in their writing.

had has	if is in	jar job	kite
H h	**I i**	**J j**	**K k**

As students repeatedly copy these words from the wall, they will become less and less dependent on looking up at them. Soon, most students will have internalized the correct spelling of the words. Once you notice that most of the students have mastered the spelling of a word, take it down to make room for another needed word.

Sample Word List

the	of	and	to	in	is	over
you	that	it	he	was	for	on
are	as	with	his	they	I	part
a	be	this	have	from	or	one
had	by	word	but	not	what	all
were	we	when	your	can	said	there
use	an	each	which	she	do	how
their	if	will	up	other	about	our
many	then	them	these	so	some	her
would	make	like	him	into	time	has
look	two	more	write	go	see	number
no	way	could	people	my	than	first

Feature Author/ Artist Bulletin Board

Featuring an author or illustrator in an area of your classroom is very motivating for the students. It allows students to enjoy the talents of creative people. This type of bulletin board teaches students to appreciate the different styles of authors and artists.

Some suggestions for this bulletin board include:

- Name of author or artist
- Facts about the person
- Interest baskets with the featured author or artist's works (Keep these interest baskets in the reading corner upon completion of featuring this author/ artist. Children will enjoy going back to familiar works and will be on the lookout for more to add to the collection.)
- Book jackets or prints of works
- Cassette tapes to accompany author's work
- Duplicated copies or pages from an author/artist's work and tracing paper (The children will trace and very closely recreate a particular drawing using various art media found in the art area.)
- A graph or tally sheet for students' critique of a book (Give two choices from which students will choose. Select, for example: *Which book do you like better?*, *Which character would you like to be?*, or *Is this book reality or fantasy?*)

Classroom Information Bulletin Board

Choose a bulletin board somewhere conspicuous in your classroom. Post important classroom management information. This information is helpful in establishing routines for children, parents, and other visitors. It is also vital information for substitute teachers.

Suggested information for the bulletin board includes:

- Emergency information including evacuation route
- Location of substitute folder
- Daily schedule
- Bell schedule
- Lunch and rainy day lunch schedule
- Class lists (without addresses and telephone numbers as these are sometimes confidential)
- Class rules or expectations
- Times that students leave the room for special services, such as speech.

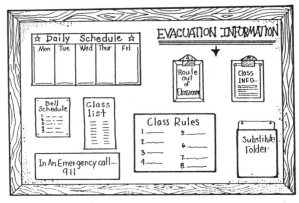

Sample Classroom Arrangement

This is a sample floor plan with the components for a whole language classroom. Modify this to match available equipment and stationary furniture.

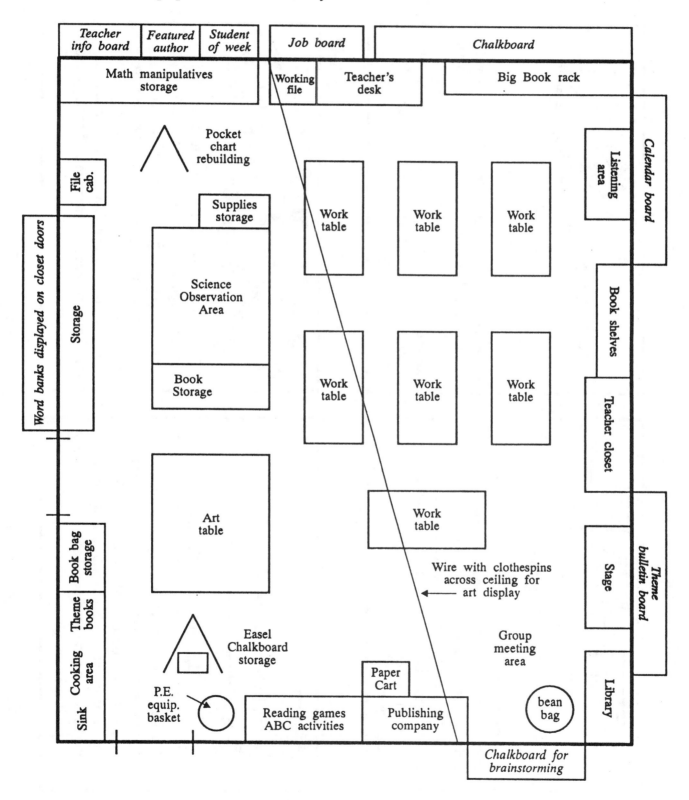

Quick and Easy Ideas

Cut out these management tips, and glue them onto index cards for easy reference.

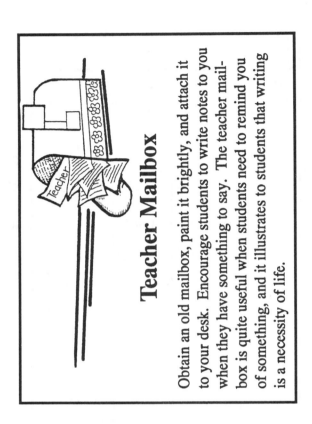

Teacher Mailbox

Obtain an old mailbox, paint it brightly, and attach it to your desk. Encourage students to write notes to you when they have something to say. The teacher mailbox is quite useful when students need to remind you of something, and it illustrates to students that writing is a necessity of life.

Baggie Books

This is a great way to make quick, reusable class books. Staple together closeable heavy-duty plastic bags on the folded ends (openings out). Use half as many bags as you have students since pages can be back-to-back. Then cover stapled edge with book tape or colored, wide plastic tape. Simply insert student-made pages. They stay clean and intact!

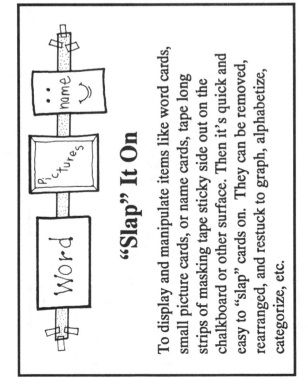

"Slap" It On

To display and manipulate items like word cards, small picture cards, or name cards, tape long strips of masking tape sticky side out on the chalkboard or other surface. Then it's quick and easy to "slap" cards on. They can be removed, rearranged, and restuck to graph, alphabetize, categorize, etc.

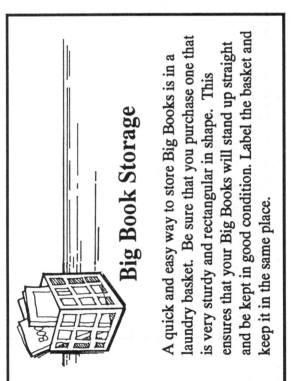

Big Book Storage

A quick and easy way to store Big Books is in a laundry basket. Be sure that you purchase one that is very sturdy and rectangular in shape. This ensures that your Big Books will stand up straight and be kept in good condition. Label the basket and keep it in the same place.

Quick and Easy Ideas *(cont.)*

Interest Baskets

Use plastic baskets as book baskets. Group books of specific topics or authors together in various centers around your room. Baskets often spark interest because children know exactly where to go back for more books about a motivating topic. It also allows for the books to be displayed cover-side out which is an exciting invitation to a child to read.

Pointer

Make a pointer available to your students during open work time. This will be used to point to and read print around the room. Be sure the pointer has a blunt or rubber tip and is used correctly. Find a convenient spot for it to be kept. This is an instant activity that the children love.

Storage Tips

Purchase flat cardboard boxes that are designed to fit under the bed for versatile storage boxes in your classroom. They are the perfect size for storage of your sentence strip stories and other pocket chart lessons. These boxes also stack nicely making them great for storage of month-specific items like Halloween bulletin boards or art projects.

To Go Home

Designate some kind of receptacle (a drawer, a tub, or a shelf) for items to go home that day. This helps assure that nothing will be forgotten during the last few hectic minutes of the school day. Mark it clearly for substitute teachers and/or parent helpers. Give the responsibility of reminding you to check it each day to a student or a pair of students so you're doubly sure that the class has been reminded.

Questions Teachers Often Ask About Whole Language Classrooms

How do I fit all these things into the day?

The day is heavily integrated so that subjects can overlap and several skills and strategies can be taught in one activity. Remember, the language arts are woven throughout the entire day, so you don't need to add up minutes and worry about whether or not you're teaching enough reading. Likewise, your reading or writing lesson is almost always centered around a content area topic.

How do I make the whole language approach understandable to parents and gain their support?

The key is making parents knowledgeable about whole language. Most non-supportive parents really don't understand what you're doing and the rationale behind it. So you must make and keep them aware of your curriculum and goals. It's great to have a parent information meeting to share your philosophy and plan for their children. Back-to-school night is usually not a sufficient amount of time. If you do attempt to explain on that occasion, be sure not to overwhelm or go too deeply into the matter. Establish an open invitation to parents to visit your classroom. Encourage them to stay for a reasonable amount of time so that they can begin to see the whole of the environment. Last, always keep communication open between home and school. Keep parents informed and ask them to advise you if a problem arises regarding your program.

Where do I get all the materials and energy it takes to set up and maintain a whole language classroom?

Realize that it takes several years of planning, trial-and-error, making, collecting, and purchasing to get to where you want your classroom to be. Ask parents and family for donations such as receptacles and books. Have them keep their eyes open for bargains and opportunities to supply your room. Make a list of materials you need and send it home. Parents are usually eager to help. The rewards and enthusiasm that grow with a whole language classroom will supply the energy you need to pull it off. Doubts and "lulls" will inevitably occur. For your emotional well-being, find a fellow teacher who shares in your endeavor and use each other for moral support and sharing.

Questions Teachers Often Ask About Whole Language Classrooms *(cont.)*

How do I know that the students are really learning and covering all the expected outcomes for their grade level?

Learning outcomes and grade level criterion vary from school to school and district to district. Be aware of your year-long goals and expectations so that you can assess throughout the year and adjust your program if necessary. Remember, general underlying goals that are difficult to measure are the most important. In reading, for instance, if your students are enjoying reading and using all of their cue systems, your program is effective. Remember, too, that results are often slow in coming, so appreciate the process and encourage students and parents to do the same! Instruction is whole class but the all-important practice, where the learning is internalized and developed, is individualized. Teachers must be sure that ample practice time is provided for each student at his/her developmental level. Feel free to work with small groups of students who are experiencing the same difficulty or require similar teacher-directed practice. Working with selected students to challenge them is also appropriate so they can practice at a higher level. There are certain measures of evaluation that must be done by teachers. Portfolio assessment should fulfill those requirements.

How do I ensure that enough phonics instruction is happening in my classroom?

Fortunately, phonics is integrated into any lesson or activity that includes print. Whenever a student is hearing sound while attending to print, phonics instruction is occurring. And it's through that repeated letter-sound association that students understand how print works. Although each day includes some formal instruction in the areas of spelling/phonics, most of the instruction happens incidentally and without the children realizing how much they are learning. You can assess students' phonics mastery in their journal entries and other writings which include invented spelling.

Is there a place for "dittoes" or worksheets anywhere in the whole language curriculum?

Paper and pencil drill activities used with purpose and in moderation, are appropriate reinforcement tools to be used after skills are presented and taught. Be sure that skills are taught in context first before being used on a worksheet.

In addition, reproducible pages can be quite useful to students in reinforcing study skills, such as staying on task, neatness and the responsibility of completing an assignment.

Bibliography

Eggelton, Jill. *Whole Language Evaluation.* (Applecross, 1990) (Distributed by the Wright Group, 1-800-523-2371)

Ferguson, M. Phyllis. Structuring the Whole Language Classroom. (Whole Language Workshops, Inc., 1988)

Gentry, J. Richard. *Spel is a Four-Letter Word.* (Heinemann, 1987) (1-800-541-2086)

Goodman, Kenneth. Lois Bridges Bird, and Yetta M. Goodman. *The Whole Language Catalog.* (American School Publishers, 1991) (1-800-882-2502)

Goodman, Ken. *What's Whole in Whole Language?* (Heinemann, 1986)

Hancock, Joelie and Susan Hill, ed. *Literature-Based Reading Programs at Work.* (Heinemann, 1988)

Kovalik, Susan. *Teachers Make the Difference.* (Susan Kovalik and Associates, 1990) (P.O. Box 29455, Village of Oak Creek, Arizona 86341)

McCracken, Robert and Marlene. *Stories, Songs & Poetry to Teach Reading & Writing.* (Peguis, 1986) (520 Hargrave St., Winnepeg, MB Canada R3A 0X8)

McCracken, Robert and Marlene. *A Practical Guide for Primary Teachers.* (Peguis, 1979)

McCracken, Robert and Marlene. *Reading is Only the Tiger's Tail.* (Peguis, 1972)

Newman, Judith M. ed. *Whole Language Theory in Use.* (Heinemann, 1985)

Pappas, Christine, Barbara Kiefer, Linda Lerstik. *An Integrated Language Perspective in the Elementary School.* (Longman, 1990) (95 Church Street, White Plains, NY 10601)

Trelease, Jim. *The New Read-Aloud Handbook.* (Penguin, 1989)

Recordings

Millang, Steve and Greg Scelsa. *We All Live Together Vol. 2.* "Months of the Year Song" (English and Spanish) (Youngheart Records, 1978)

Millang, Steve and Greg Scelsa. *We All Live Together Vol. 4.* "Days of the Week" (English and Spanish) (Youngheart Records, 1987)